Super Smart Animals

Horses
Are Smart!

Leigh Rockwood

PowerKiDS
press™
New York

Published in 2010 by The Rosen Publishing Group, Inc.
29 East 21st Street, New York, NY 10010

First Edition

Editor: Amelie von Zumbusch
Book Design: Julio Gil
Photo Researcher: Jessica Gerweck

Photo Credits: Cover, back cover (dolphin, horse, parrot, pig), pp. 5, 9, 10, 13, 14, 17, 21 Shutterstock. com; back cover (chimpanzee) Manoj Shah/Getty Images; back cover (dog) Courtesy of Lindsy Whitten; p. 6 Eastcott Momatiuk/Getty Images; p. 18 Thomas Northcut/Getty Images.

Library of Congress Cataloging-in-Publication Data

Rockwood, Leigh.
 Horses are smart! / Leigh Rockwood. — 1st ed.
    p. cm. — (Super smart animals)
Includes index.
 ISBN 978-1-4358-9399-3 (library binding) — ISBN 978-1-4358-9838-7 (pbk.) —
ISBN 978-1-4358-9839-4 (6-pack)
 1. Horses—Juvenile literature. 2. Horses—Psychology—Juvenile literature. I. Title.
SF302.R626 2010
636.1—dc22
                    2009033096

Manufactured in the United States of America

CPSIA Compliance Information: Batch #WW10PK: For Further Information contact Rosen Publishing, New York, New York at 1-800-237-9932

Contents

The Helpful Horse

Horses have played an important part in human history. Horses were first **domesticated** in Asia over 4,000 years ago. Today, they live all around the world. In the past, people used horses to pull carts and wagons. People have ridden horses onto countless battlefields, too. For much of history, riding horses was among the main ways people traveled over long distances.

Horses have played so many roles in people's lives, not only because they are strong and fast, but also because they are smart. Their skill at learning **behaviors** and commands makes them perfect for many different jobs.

Since horses are smart, they can be trained to follow a rider's commands. Riders often direct horses to jump over bars, gates, and other objects on riding courses. ▶

Horse Breeds

There is only one **species** of horse. Within the species are around 400 different horse **breeds**. The Thoroughbred is a well-known racing breed. The Clydesdale is a breed known for its strength. Clydesdales often pull heavy carts and wagons.

Although most horses today live with people on farms, there are small herds, or groups, that live in the wild. Mustangs are among the best-known of these horses. They live in the western United States. Przewalski's horse is a breed of wild horse that lived in Mongolia, in Asia, for thousands of years. Today, this breed is found only in zoos.

◀ **These mustangs live in the hills of Montana's Pryor Mountain Wild Horse Range. This park is home to more than 100 mustangs.**

A Show of Hands

Horses are **mammals** with rounded bodies, four long legs, and large heads. These large animals also have tails and manes. Horses can be many colors, such as brown, black, white, reddish orange, or a mix of these colors. Horses have good hearing. They also have great eyesight. They can see clearly in very low light. Horses' eyes can even move separately from each other!

A horse's height is measured in hands from the ground to its withers, or shoulder. A hand is 4 inches (10 cm) long. An adult horse can be anywhere from 7.2 to 17 hands tall.

Along with different colors, horses' coats can have different markings. Some horses, such as the one here, have spots.

A Horse's Life Cycle

Horses live for 25 to 35 years. These animals go by many names during their lives. Baby horses are foals. When they are between one and two years old, horses are yearlings. Males between one and four years old are called colts, while females are fillies. Beyond four years of age, males are stallions and females are mares.

Horses reach adulthood at two years of age and are able to **mate**. A mother horse gives birth to one foal, which she **nurses** for seven months. Foals get on the move quickly. They can stand and follow their mothers just half an hour after they were born!

◄ As adult horses do, foals need to get exercise every day. These growing horses should have plenty of room to run and play.

Grazing and Herd Life

Horses are **herbivores**. They eat both grasses and grains. Horses often graze, or feed on growing grasses. A horse eats around 20 pounds (9 kg) of food and drinks about 8 gallons (30 l) of water every day. Horses are active animals. They need large, fenced-in fields in which to run and graze.

In the wild, horses live in herds of 3 to 20 animals. A herd is made up of a stallion, a group of mares, and their young. Female horses generally stay with the same herd their whole lives. However, young males leave the herd when they become adults. They stick together as a group until each male gathers its own group of mares.

You can see horses of many different ages and sizes in this herd. Herds are generally led by one of the group's older mares. ▶

Horse Talk

Horses **communicate** with each other using scent, sound, and body language. Horses depend on scent when they greet each other. They touch noses and puff air at each other's **nostrils**. Horses also make neighing and whinnying noises. These noises can have many different tones, which help horses communicate different moods.

Scientists have done studies to measure how smart horses are. They try to figure out how many tasks horses can learn, how fast they learn them, and how well they remember them. Since horses are best at communicating through body language, people have come up with training methods that use this skill.

◀ **These foals are rubbing noses. Rubbing noses is also known as nuzzling. It is a sign that the two horses are friends.**

Riding Horses

Today, many horses are trained for the sport of horseback riding. In this sport, people direct horses to follow courses and to move at different speeds. The speeds, from slowest to fastest, are walking, trotting, cantering, and galloping. There are also jumping contests in which horses jump over fences.

Riders use special **equipment** to ride a horse. The bit rests in the horse's mouth. It connects to a bridle, which holds the reins the rider pulls on to direct the horse. Riders sit in a saddle with their feet in stirrups. This helps riders **balance** in the saddle and use their legs to command the horse.

This young rider is wearing a riding hat. Riding hats have a hard inside. They keep a rider's head safe if the rider falls off or is thrown from a horse. ▶

Horse Training

Horses are trained using methods that make the most of their intelligence. Horses have good hearing and a great memory. A style of teaching called conditioning allows riders to use these talents to teach horses commands.

In conditioning, riders give each command not only by saying it, but also by shifting in the saddle, moving their legs, or pulling on the reins. The rider repeats the command until the horse gets it right. As soon as the horse gets the command right, the rider gives the horse praise. Riders often praise horses by petting them or by saying "good."

◄ **This woman is training the horse shown here. Horse trainers need to be firm and gentle so that they do not scare these big, powerful animals.**

Hardworking Horses

The fact that horses are strong, fast, and easy to train makes them suited for many jobs. For example, some horses are police horses or search-and-rescue horses. Police horses help officers work in large crowds. These horses go through training to make them comfortable being among crowds and to keep them calm around loud noises. This training can go on for up to three years.

Search-and-rescue teams use horses to help them search for people who are lost in the wilderness. People on horses can cover large areas much faster than people on foot can. Horses must be healthy and calm to be part of a rescue team.

Police horses often wear visors, like the ones in this photo, over their eyes. They help keep the animals' eyes from getting hurt while the horses are working. ▶

New Jobs for Horses

As we begin to understand more about how horses learn, we have discovered new ways to make them part of our lives. Their intelligence makes horses suited for a growing list of jobs.

One new job for horses is being guides for the blind. **Miniature** horses are used for this. As all horses are, miniature horses are gentle, trainable, and great at remembering how to get to different places. At about 26 inches (66 cm) tall at the shoulder, miniature horses are also the perfect size for being a guide animal. Who knows what other useful jobs horses may fill in the years to come?

Glossary

balance (BAL-ens) To stay steady.

behaviors (bee-HAY-vyurz) Ways to act.

breeds (BREEDZ) Groups of animals that look alike and have the same relatives.

communicate (kuh-MYOO-nih-kayt) To share facts or feelings.

domesticated (duh-MES-tih-kayt-id) Raised to live with people.

equipment (uh-KWIP-mint) All the supplies needed to do something.

herbivores (ER-buh-vorz) Animals that eat plants.

mammals (MA-mulz) Warm-blooded animals that have backbones and hair, breathe air, and feed milk to their young.

mate (MAYT) To join together to make babies.

miniature (MIH-nee-uh-chur) Very small.

nostrils (NOS-trulz) The openings to the nose.

nurses (NURS-ez) When a female feeds her baby milk from her body.

species (SPEE-sheez) One kind of living thing. All people are one species.

Index

A

Asia, 4, 7

B

battlefields, 4
behaviors, 4
breed(s), 7

C

carts, 4, 7
Clydesdale(s), 7
command(s), 4, 16, 19

E

equipment, 16

F

foal(s), 11

H

herbivores, 12
history, 4

J

job(s), 4, 20, 22

M

mammals, 8

N

nostrils, 15

P

people, 4, 7, 15, 16, 20

R

riders, 16, 19

S

skill, 4, 15
species, 7

T

Thoroughbred, 7

W

wagons, 4, 7

Web Sites

Due to the changing nature of Internet links, PowerKids Press has developed an online list of Web sites related to the subject of this book. This site is updated regularly. Please use this link to access the list: www.powerkidslinks.com/ssan/horse/